Hans W. Liebheit

Ices
and Sorbets

Cookery Editor Sonia Allison

Series Editor Wendy Hobson

foulsham

Foreword

There are few greater pleasures in life than eating ice cream. It cools down the soul on hot summer days better than almost anything else. And winter makes little difference as ice cream sits beside portions of hot apple pie, sticky jam roll or is itself cascading with hot sauces like fudges, chocolate or mocha.

Interestingly, the best ice cream is said to come from Russia and Poland, where it is made from pure ingredients and is satin smooth and blissfully chewy. One of the strangest sights in the winter, at least to a stranger, is to watch the locals queuing up at kiosks in heavy boots and fur hats, tramping through the snow with huge cones of ice cream to savour en route to their destinations.

Supermarkets and freezer centres have made life easy by stocking ice cream throughout the year and we have a vast choice of family-priced cartons with glamorous luxury ones alongside frivolous, confections for dessert, but once you have made your own ice creams and sorbets you will find that the flavours are so wonderful that you will want to enjoy their pleasures again and again.

Contents

4

Cool Temptations for Any Time of Day

Since the beginning of the nineteenth century, hardly any other form of refreshment has been greeted with as much pleasure as ice cream by young and old alike. And its popularity is set to continue.

Many ice creams are available in the shops, but you will find that the tastiest ice creams are those you make yourself with fresh cream, milk, eggs and fruits.

5

The History of Ice Cream

We have the Chinese to thank for inventing porcelain, tea-drinking, fireworks and ice mixtures – the ancient forerunners of modern ice creams and sorbets. Well over 500 years ago, the Chinese made up a mixture of chopped ice and fruit for summer eating and the philosopher Confucius was said to have been very partial to this hot-weather delicacy.

In Ancient Greece, it is said that Orpheus, subject of so many apocryphal stories, cooled himself with a mixture of snow, honey, fruit juices and chopped fruit after his return from the heat of the underworld. And it is said of Hippocrates that he prescribed 'something icy' to many of his patients who were tired of life.

In Ancient Rome, the enjoyment of natural ice was common and the Romans often used ice for cooling drinks. Even the famous historian Pliny wrote about it: 'One drinks ice, another snow. Ice is saved for the summer and a way has even been found to make ice in the hottest months of the year.' The manufacture of ice has even been described by the Emperor Nero. He is said to have boiled water and then put the pan into ice in order to freeze it. This makes him Italy's first 'gelatieri'!

Around the end of the thirteenth century, the Italian explorer Marco Polo brought ice recipes from distant China to Venice. The Arabs, too, had a type of ice cream called sherbet, the forerunner of our modern sorbet.

Ice came to Sicily from the Orient. If the Italians cannot take the full credit for actually inventing ice cream, they certainly vastly improved its quality. It was a Sicilian who, in 1530, cleverly added saltpetre to the frozen substance, a process that has remained with us to the present day.

From Italy, the art of preparing ice cream moved with Catherine de Medici to France. In 1651, the Sicilian nobleman Francesco Procopio de Coltelli opened the first ice cream café in the Rue des Fosses in Paris. Other ice cream cafés followed. They became well known and well patronised by the

rich and for over a century, Paris was the ice cream capital of Europe. The triumphant advance of ice cream seemed unstoppable and Casanova appeared to have been almost as much in love with this latest confection as he was with his women. In his memoirs, he recalls a garden party at which a range of wonderful ice creams were on offer to delight the guests. Lemon ice cream was served in the shape of a lemon; coffee and chocolate ice creams were served in shell-shaped dishes of ice – a typical Italian way of presentation.

At this time, the French scientist Réamur discovered that ice cream tasted better if it was stirred frequently during freezing. This constituted a revolution in ice cream-making and led to the invention of the ice cream machine. Called a sabotière, it remained almost unchanged until this century, and even today it is possible to find machines that work on the same principle as the original sabotières. A tightly closed container is inserted into a larger container filled with blocks of ice and salt. The ice cream mixture is placed in the central container,

which can then be stirred with a whisk inserted through a hole in the lid. The more the ice cream is stirred, the creamier and softer it becomes.

In 1794, ice cream was introduced to the New World by an immigrant named Collet, a Frenchman who made a fortune selling a variety of ice creams made with fruit.

Around the middle of the eighteenth century, the poor inhabitants of two valleys in the Italian Dolomite mountains started to take ice cream with them in the summer when going walking. About 1865 – so it is recorded – the authorities in Vienna gave permission to Tomea Antonio Bareta to have a permanent pitch for his ice cream cart in the Prater in Vienna. Throughout the following years, more and more 'gelatieri' moved from their homes in the Dolomites to northern Europe, and before the First World War, every large town in Europe boasted Italian ice cream shops.

At the time when the inhabitants of the Dolomites first began to sell their ice cream in northern Europe, a mechanised ice cream machine was invented in America. With this invention, began the industrial manufacture of ice cream and soon this became part and parcel of the American way of life. In no other country in the world is so much ice cream consumed per head of population. On average, every American gets through 24 litres of ice cream every year – around 850 million scoops in all.

Those who think that most ice cream is eaten only in hot countries are mistaken. The Russians, the British, the Irish, Danes and Swiss are all enthusiastic consumers, and the Swedes now eat more than the Italians.

In southern Europe – in Spain, Italy and Portugal – there is another particular ice dessert known as granita. This is a lightly sweetened water ice left to freeze with minimal stirring so that it has a granular texture and melts quickly. It is the perfect dessert for a hot summer day.

Down through the ages, culinary artists have dedicated their creations to the rich and famous. Auguste Escoffier designed peach melba for the famous Australian singer Helen Porter-Mitchell who called herself Nellie Melba, and a strawberry on pineapple ice cream with frozen Curaçao mousse was named after the actress Sarah Bernhardt.

Basic Ices

Basically, ice creams are made from sugar, milk, eggs, as well as natural flavourings. For quality it should contain about 270 g/9 oz whole eggs or 100 g/4 oz egg yolks to every litre/1³/₄ pt/4¹/₄ cups of milk.

Fruit ice cream is made from sugar, water, fresh fruit, fruit purée or juice and should have at least 20 per cent fruit, the only exception being lemon ice cream with just 10 per cent.

Cream ice is made of sugar and whipped cream as well as natural flavouring, scented ingredients and should contain at least 60 per cent cream.

From these three basic types it is possible to make any number of variations.

Making Ice Cream
First of all, a few words about making the different types of ice cream. You will soon discover that each type is made from a basic mixture – with many variations, but otherwise with the same ingredients. This means that parfaits should, for authenticity, always contain cream and milk. For the best results, always use the freshest and highest quality ingredients.

Ice Cream
Egg yolk and sugar are beaten until fluffy. The milk is combined with cream and heated with the flavouring. The egg yolk mixture and hot milk are whisked in a bowl over a saucepan of simmering water and gently beaten until cold. The mixture is then put into a dish, covered and frozen. During the freezing process, the mixture must be briskly stirred a number of times to ensure smoothness and prevent crystallisation and a grainy texture.

Parfait
The aristocratic variation of ice cream is made from egg yolk and cream combined with sugar syrup and flavouring. In a bowl set over a saucepan of

simmering water, the sugar syrup and egg yolk are whipped to a thick cream and then whipped gently until cold. The flavouring is added and the whipped cream carefully folded in. Afterwards the mixture is put into a mould or bowl, covered and frozen. Because it contains a large amount of egg yolk and cream, stirring whilst freezing is unnecessary. Also the time of freezing is shorter (about 2 to 3 hours). I therefore recommend that a parfait is prepared just a few hours before serving.

Fruit Ice
The simple, quickly prepared fruit ice is made of fresh fruit, sugar syrup and a little lemon juice to stabilise and contain the taste of the fruit. The fruit itself is converted into a fine purée in a blender. The sugar syrup and lemon juice are mixed into the purée, which is then transferred to a bowl, covered and frozen. It is important to stir the mixture briskly several times during freezing to prevent the formation of large ice crystals.

Sorbet
This variation of fruit ice is made from thin fruit purée combined with clarified sugar and lemon juice or liqueur, Champagne or wine. The ice mixture is either put into a sorbetière, or it must – this is very important – be stirred frequently to achieve a smooth consistency. Whereas ice cream, parfaits and fruit ices are served in scoops or twirls, sorbet is usually spooned or piped into a glass.

Ice Bombes
An ice bombe is made of two types of ice cream filled into a half-round mould. The outer coat is made of ice cream fruit ice (a chilled mould is filled to about 1 cm/¹/₂ in thickness with ice cream), and the filling comprises a parfait mixture. To serve, the bombe is dipped into

warm water, removed from its mould and decorated.

Ice Cream Gâteau
Freezing an ice cream gâteau is best done in a spring clip cake tin. The base, usually a sponge cake, is soaked in flavoured sugar syrup and filled with ice cream or fruit ice. Also a parfait mixture can be used as a filling.

Notes on the Recipes

1 Follow one set of measurements only, do not mix metric and Imperial.
2 Eggs are size 2.
3 Wash fresh produce before preparation.
4 Spoon measurements are level.
5 Kcals are for the dish and are approximate.
6 Preparation times and freezing times are approximate.

Equipment

Top quality ingredients and the right equipment help the domestic cook to achieve success. The following is a guide to what you will need.

An ice cream machine with a capacity of one kilo/2 lb or more, available from stores and kitchen shops, may be very practical but is quite expensive to buy. The same results can be achieved on a smaller scale using a sorbetière. Whereas an ice cream machine does not need external cooling, a sorbetière must be put into the freezer compartment of a refrigerator or in a deep freezer. The built-in electrical mechanism stirs the ice cream mixture periodically for you.

For anyone not wishing to purchase an ice cream or a sorbetière, home-made ice cream can still be made in a container in the freezing compartment of a refrigerator. It is important that the refrigerator or deep freezer is turned to its coldest setting and that there is no food near the ice cream with a strong flavour.

Besides whisks and blenders, a good range of bowls are vital for both making and freezing the ice cream. For this purpose metal containers are the most suitable as they conduct the cold more efficiently and you can easily buy many different kinds and in all shapes and sizes. Straightforward plastic dishes, however, serve the same purpose, so there is no point in investing heavily in savarin tins, ornate moulds and other additions unless you plan on making ice cream frequently.

Ingredients

Always use fresh eggs. A fresh egg can be judged by its yolk. When broken on to a plate, it should stand up like a dome and the surrounding white should look almost gelatinous. Stale whites rarely beat up satisfactorily.

Always use caster sugar or icing sugar. Vanilla sugar can be made by storing a vanilla pod in a screw-top jar of caster sugar. The flavour will become stronger the longer the jar is left. For some recipes, you will need sugar syrup, the recipe for which you will find on page 16.

Milk, cream and yoghurt must be fresh and well chilled before use. The richer the products, the richer the ice cream.

Best quality fruit is essential and only fresh, ripe and perfect fruit make the best tasting fruit ice or sorbet. Fruit pulp and purée can be prepared in advance and kept in a covered container in the freezer.

Liqueur, brandy, armagnac, rum or fruit brandies add to the flavour of your ice cream considerably — in taste as well as in texture. You may find it convenient to buy a few miniature bottles for your ice cream-making if you do not usually keep liqueurs.

Almonds and other nuts should be used freshly shelled whenever possible. When nuts are bought in packets, check the sell-by date as stale ones will spoil the flavour of your ice cream. Roast the nuts and almonds just before use in a dry frying pan. This brings out the full flavour and aroma.

Serving Ice Cream

For novelty, offer your ice cream as the Romans did in their day – in fruit shells. For pineapple ice cream, for example, slice off the top of the pineapple and remove the flesh carefully from inside, leaving a perfect container. Melons, paw-paws and kiwi fruits are also suitable. You can use citrus fruits, too, but take care not to place the ice cream in the peel cases more than an hour or so before serving otherwise the bitter juices in the peel may affect the flavour.

Sauces

It is well worth preparing different sauces to serve with your ice creams.

Fruit sauces are quick and easy to make and can be kept for some time in the refrigerator. Fresh soft fruits such as strawberries, raspberries, mangoes and kiwi fruit can be quickly puréed in a mixer and then combined with sugar to taste and a little lemon juice and flavoured with a shot of liqueur, rum or brandy. A little whipped cream, stirred into the purée, enriches the taste.

When serving ice cream with sauces, you can also enhance the presentation of your desserts. If you freeze your nougat ice cream in a block-shaped mould, it can be served sliced on to a flat plate with a few spoonfuls of raspberry sauce flooded on to the plate and garnished with raspberries.

You can make a vanilla sauce in the same way as vanilla ice cream but reducing the amount of cream. The same goes for chocolate and nougat sauces.

Sprinklers

It is nice to serve a selection of accompaniments for guests to sprinkle on to their ice cream, for example: lightly toasted coconut, grated chocolate, drinking chocolate powder, chopped nuts, coarsely chopped ginger biscuits, chocolate chips.

Ice Bombes and Gâteaux

Visually impressive, these can be made quite simply from a coating or overcoat of frozen ice cream with a filling of a parfait mixture. For success, you do need time, patience and either a bombe mould or a pudding basin – any utensil that is half a sphere. First, thoroughly chill the bowl. Make the ice cream and spoon it into the base and sides of the dish then freeze it for about 1 hour until firmly set and hard. Fill the inside with a second ice cream or parfait mixture, cover and deep-freeze until solid.

To serve, dip the mould in and out of hot water for a few seconds then invert on to a serving plate.

You can use any basic ice cream recipe for the outside of the mould. The filling inside can be parfait or the bombe filling below. You can also fill the mould with fruit if you wish, but it should first be dipped in sugar syrup to prevent it from over-freezing and becoming too hard to eat. The flavours of the coating and filling should be complementary. Suggested combinations are almond-rum, mocha-vanilla, cracknell-strawberry, chocolate-kirsch, vanilla-maraschino.

Bombe Filling

175 ml/6 fl oz/³⁄₄ cup sugar syrup (page 16)
4 egg yolks
300 ml/¹⁄₂ pt/1 ¹⁄₄ cups double cream
flavouring to taste

Whisk together the hot sugar syrup and egg yolks until fluffy. In a separate bowl, whip the cream until thick. Gradually fold in the egg yolk mixture and flavour.

Cream Ices,
Fruit Ices
and Bombes

Spoil yourself and your family and guests by making home-made smooth traditional ice creams which are perfect for every day, or can be beautifully presented to round off the best dinner party.

Sugar Syrup

Makes 600 ml/1 pt/2½ cups
Preparation time: 30 mins plus chilling

1.5 kg/3¼ lb/6½ cups caster sugar
450 ml/¾ pt/2 cups water

1 Put the sugar and water in a saucepan and stir over a very low heat until the sugar has dissolved.
2 Bring the mixture to the boil and skim off the froth.
3 As soon as the froth stops forming, leave to cool.
4 Chill the sugar syrup and store in an air-tight jar in the refrigerator.

Strawberry Fruit Ice

Serves 8
Preparation time: 15 mins
Freezing time: 3 hrs
2190 kcal/9160 kJ

450 g/1 lb strawberries
450 ml/¾ pt/2 cups Sugar Syrup (page 16)
10 ml/2 tsp lemon juice

1 Purée the strawberries then mix them with the cold sugar syrup. Add the lemon juice, pour into a mould, cover and freeze.
2 During freezing, stir the mixture vigorously every 30 minutes.

Photograph opposite (centre)

Blackcurrant Fruit Ice Cream

Serves 8
Preparation time: 45 mins
Freezing time: 4 hours
1360 kcal/5690 kJ

450 g/1 lb blackcurrants or bilberries
20 ml/4 tsp water
250 ml/8 fl oz/1 cup Sugar Syrup (page 16)
10 ml/2 tsp lemon juice
5 ml/1 tsp vanilla essence
2 egg whites

1 Remove the berries from the stalks and simmer with the water over a low heat until soft. Rub through a fine sieve.
2 Combine the fruit purée with sugar syrup and lemon juice. Add the vanilla essence. Pour into a freezer container and freeze for 30 minutes.
3 Whisk the egg whites until quite stiff then fold into the frozen ice. Leave until it is completely frozen, stirring frequently.
4 About 15 minutes before using, transfer to the refrigerator to soften.

Photograph opposite (bottom)

Pineapple Fruit Ice

Serves 8
Preparation time: 40 mins
Freezing time: 6 hours
3250 kcal/13600 kJ

1 fresh pineapple
750 ml/1¼ pts/3 cups Sugar Syrup (page 16)
1 egg white
a pinch of salt

1 Peel the pineapple, remove the miniature brown 'cores' then chop up the fruit, reserving the juice. Purée both fruit and juice in a blender then combine it with the Sugar Syrup.
2 Transfer to a freezer container and freeze for 3 hours stirring frequently.
3 Whisk the egg whites and salt until stiff and fold smoothly into the mixture. Freeze the mixture again for 3 hours. About 10 minutes before serving, transfer to the refrigerator to soften.
4 As a variation, make by using about 500 g/1¼ lb stoned apricots instead of pineapple.

Photograph opposite (top)

17

Blackberry Ice Cream

Serves 6
Preparation time: 45 mins
Freezing time: 4 hours
1940 kcal/8120 kJ

400 g/*14 oz* blackberries
15 ml/*1 tbsp* caster sugar
120 ml/*4 fl oz*/¹/₂ cup water
40 g/1¹/₂ *oz*/3 tbsp sugar
3 egg yolks
15 ml/*1 tbsp* icing sugar
15 ml/*1 tbsp* cherry liqueur
450 ml/³/₄ *pt*/2 cups double cream, whipped

1 Simmer the blackberries and caster sugar over a low heat for about 10 minutes until softened. Rub through a sieve and leave to cool.
2 Heat the water with the sugar in a pan and stir continuously until the sugar dissolves. Boil over a brisk heat until the syrup pulls up into threads. Leave to cool a little.
3 Whisk the sugar syrup with the egg yolks until fluffy. Mix the icing sugar with the cherry liqueur and purée then gradually add the whisked egg. Fold in the whipped cream. Pour into a mould, cover and freeze.
4 An hour before serving, transfer to the refrigerator to soften.

Photograph (left)

Orange Ice Cream

Serves 4
Preparation time: 45 mins
Freezing time: 3 hours
2310 kcal/9665 kJ

---

2 large oranges

grated rind of 2 oranges

*100 g/**4 oz**/¹/₂ cup caster sugar*

4 egg yolks

*300 ml/¹/₂ **pt**/¹/₄ cups single cream*

*150 ml/¹/₄ **pt**/²/₃ cup double cream, whipped*

---

1 Halve the oranges and remove the flesh, reserving the juice. Purée the fruit then rub it through a sieve.
2 Mix the orange rind, sugar and egg yolks well. Whisk with an electric mixer until thick. Warm up the single cream, but do not let it boil. Stir it into the egg yolk mixture.
3 Continue stirring the mixture in a bowl over a pan of warm water until thick. Add the orange juice then rub through a sieve. Leave to cool.
4 Fold the orange and egg mixture into the double cream, turn into a ring mould, cover and freeze until hard.

Photograph (right)

Gourmet Tip
Serve the ice cream with thin orange slices marinated in Grand Marnier.

Marzipan Ice

Serves 4
Preparation time: 1 hour
Freezing time: 3 hours
2120 kcal/8870 kJ

100 g/4 oz/$\frac{1}{2}$ cup caster
sugar

3 egg whites

120 ml/4 fl oz/$\frac{1}{2}$ cup milk

$\frac{1}{2}$ vanilla pod

50 g/2 oz marzipan

100 g/4 oz/1 cup flaked
almonds

30 ml/1 tbsp Amaretto
liqueur

150 ml/$\frac{1}{4}$ pt/1$\frac{1}{4}$ cups
double cream, whipped

1 Beat the sugar and the
egg whites in a mixer until
creamy. Bring the milk to
the boil with the vanilla
pod. Leave to stand for
about 10 minutes then
discard the vanilla. Cut
the marzipan into small
pieces and dissolve in the
hot milk, stirring all the
time.
2 Combine the marzipan-
milk with the egg mixture.
Pour into a bowl and
immerse in a sink or larger
bowl partially filled with
cold water. Stir the mixture
until cold.
3 Lightly toast the
almonds in a frying pan
then add them to the ice
cream mixture. Stir in the
Amaretto liqueur and fold
in the cream.
4 Spoon the mixture into
individual moulds, cover
and freeze.

*Photograph opposite
(left)*

Gooseberry Kiwi Ice Cream

Serves 4
Preparation time: 45 mins
Freezing time: 4 hours
1600 kcal/6695 kJ

200 g/7 oz kiwi fruit

300 g/10 oz gooseberries,
topped and tailed

100 g/4 oz/$\frac{1}{2}$ cup caster
sugar

30 ml/2 tbsp water

4 egg whites

75 g/3 oz/$\frac{1}{3}$ cup icing
sugar

150 ml/$\frac{1}{4}$ pt/$\frac{2}{3}$ cup double
cream, whipped

1 Peel the kiwi fruit and
cut into pieces. Place in a
saucepan with the goose-
berries, sugar and water.
Cover and simmer for
about 15 minutes. Purée
whilst still warm, rub
through a sieve and leave
to cool.
2 Whisk the egg whites
until stiff, sieving in the
icing sugar a little at a time
as you do it. Mix the kiwi
fruit and gooseberry
purée with the cream and
fold in the whisked egg
whites.
3 Pour into a mould, cover
and freeze. Transfer to the
refrigerator 30 minutes
before serving to soften.

*Photograph opposite
(centre)*

Honey Ice Cream

Serves 6
Preparation time: 40 mins
Freezing time: 3 hours
1440 kcal/6025 kJ

4 egg yolks

45 ml/3 tbsp caster sugar

5 ml/1 tsp vanilla essence

2 egg whites

a pinch of salt

90 ml/6 tbsp honey

200 ml/7 fl oz/scant 1 cup
double cream, whipped

1 Whisk the egg yolk with
the sugar and vanilla
essence to a creamy mix-
ture in a bowl standing
over a pan of simmering
water. Remove from the
heat and immerse the
bowl in a sink or larger
bowl partially filled with
cold water. Beat until cool.
2 Beat the egg whites
with the salt until stiff. Fold
into the egg yolk mixture.
3 Slightly warm the honey
until it is runny and stir it
into the mixture. Carefully
fold in the cream.
4 Pour the ice mixture into
individual moulds, cover
and freeze until firm.

*Photograph opposite
(right)*

> **Gourmet Tip**
> Honey ice cream
> tastes particularly
> good served on a
> large flat plate with
> home-made fruits
> preserved in rum.

21

Coconut Ice Cream

Serves 6
Preparation time: 45 mins
Freezing time: 3 hours
1270 kcal/5315 kJ

---

50 g/*2 oz*/¹/₂ cup
desiccated coconut

---

250 ml/*8 fl oz*/1 cup coconut
milk

---

250 ml/*8 fl oz*/1 cup full
cream milk

---

4 egg yolks

---

100 g/*4 oz*/¹/₂ cup sugar

---

1 Simmer the coconut in the coconut milk for 15 minutes over a low heat. Add the milk, stir well and bring briefly to the boil.
2 Beat together the egg yolks and sugar in a bowl until foamy. Add the warm milk, stirring all the time. Place the bowl over a pan of simmering water. Beat until thick and creamy. Immerse the bowl in cold water and continue to whisk the ice cream mixture until cold.
3 Spoon into individual moulds, cover and freeze. Stir the mixture well every 30 minutes while freezing for smoothness.

Photograph (left)

Gourmet Tip
Serve sprinkled with coconut and garnished with a few slices of fresh coconut or apple.

Nougat Ice Cream

Serves 4 to 6
Preparation time: 40 mins
Freezing time: 3 hours
1900 kcal/7900 kJ

*250 ml/**8 fl oz**/1 cup full cream milk*
*150 g/**5 oz** praline chocolates*
*15 ml/**1 tbsp** ground almonds*
4 egg yolks
*15 ml/**1 tbsp** honey*
2 egg whites
*5 ml/**1 tsp** lemon juice*
*15 ml/**1 tbsp** caster sugar*
*120 ml/**4 fl oz**/¹/₂ cup double cream, whipped*

1 Heat up the milk slowly. Cut chocolates into small pieces and add to the milk with the almonds. Stir thoroughly over a moderate heat for 5 minutes. Leave until lukewarm.
2 Beat the egg yolks with the honey until creamy. Add the praline milk and pour into a bowl standing over a pan of gently simmering water. Beat until thick and creamy. Stand the bowl in a sink or larger bowl partially filled with very cold water and continue to beat until cold.
3 Beat the egg whites with the lemon juice until stiff then beat in the sugar. Fold smoothly into the egg yolk and milk mixture with the cream. Spoon into individual moulds, cover and freeze until firm.

Photograph (right)

23

Chocolate Ice Cream

Serves 4
Preparation time: 40 mins
Freezing time: 3 hours
1220 kcal/5105 kJ

75 g/3 oz dark chocolate

120 ml/4 fl oz/¹/₂ cup cream

120 ml/4 fl oz/¹/₂ cup full cream milk

15 ml/1 tbsp caster sugar

3 eggs

15 ml/1 tbsp brandy

1 Melt the chocolate in a bowl over a pan of simmering water. Meanwhile, slowly heat up the cream with the milk and half the sugar. Stir in melted chocolate.
2 Whisk the eggs, the remaining sugar and the brandy over a saucepan of simmering water. Slowly stir in the chocolate milk. Pour into a saucepan.
3 Stir over a medium heat until the mixture is creamy, rub through a sieve and leave to cool.
4 Spoon into a mould, cover and freeze. Using a fork or a hand whisk, stir frequently while freezing for smoothness.

Photograph opposite (top left)

Vanilla Ice Cream

Serves 4
Preparation time: 45 mins
Freezing time: 3 hours
1050 kcal/4400 kJ

120 ml/4 fl oz/¹/₂ cup double cream

120 ml/4 fl oz/¹/₂ cup full cream milk

2 vanilla pods

50 g/2 oz/¹/₄ cup caster sugar

4 egg yolks

1 Bring the cream, milk and vanilla pods slowly to the boil in a pan. Stir half the sugar into the hot milk. Remove the vanilla pods.
2 Meanwhile, whisk the egg yolks and the remaining sugar in a bowl over a pan of simmering water until thick. Fold the vanilla milk into the whisked egg and return to the pan.
3 Stir over a medium heat until the mixture is thick and creamy. Rub through a sieve and leave to cool.
4 Spoon into a freezer container, cover and freeze, stirring frequently until firm.

Photograph opposite (top right)

Rum and Raisin Ice Cream

Serves 4 to 6
Preparation time: 50 mins
Freezing time: 4 hours
2745 kcal/11485 kJ

75 g/3 oz/¹/₂ cup raisins

30 ml/2 tbsp rum

30 ml/2 tbsp Madeira or port

3 egg yolks

100 g/4 oz/¹/₂ cup caster sugar

600 ml/1 pt/2¹/₂ cups double cream

1 Soak the raisins in the rum and Madeira or port until soft. Whisk the egg yolks in a bowl with the sugar until fluffy.
2 Put half the cream into a pan and heat up to just below boiling point. Stir immediately into the egg mixture. Whisk the contents of the bowl over a saucepan of hot water until creamy. Rub through a sieve and leave to cool.
3 Whip the rest of the cream until stiff, fold into the warm egg yolk mixture and transfer to a rigid container. Cover and freeze for 2 to 3 hours.
4 As soon as the ice cream has frozen about 2 to 3 cm/1 to 1¹/₂ in, stir gently round and fold in the raisins with the alcohol. Leave to finish freezing.

Photograph opposite (bottom)

25

Cassata Neopolitan

Serves 8
Preparation time: 40 mins
Freezing time: 4 hours
2670 kcal/11170 kJ

---

*250 ml/**8 fl oz**/1 cup
Strawberry Fruit Ice (page
16)*

---

*250 ml/**8 fl oz**/1 cup Lime
Parfait (page 44)*

---

*250 ml/**8 fl oz**/1 cup double
cream, whipped*

---

*30 ml/**2 tbsp** candied
angelica, finely chopped*

---

*30 ml/**2 tbsp** cherries, finely
chopped*

---

*50 g/ 2 oz/$^1/_2$ cup pistachio
nuts, finely chopped*

---

1 Put a bombe mould in
the freezer for 15 minutes.
Stir the strawberry fruit ice
with a hand whisk until
soft. Using a palette knife,
spread a 1 cm/$^1/_2$ in thick
layer inside the mould
then freeze for 45 minutes.
2 Stir the lime parfait
lightly with a fork and
apply a second layer
about 2 cm/1 in thick
inside the strawberry ice.
Freeze for 45 minutes.
3 Just before the end of
the freezing time, mix the
chilled whipped cream
with the chopped fruit and
pistachio nuts. Pack into
the mould, cover and
freeze for a further 2
hours.
4 To unmould and serve,
hold the mould briefly in
warm water and tip it out
onto a well-chilled plate.

Photograph (left)

Hawaiian Ice Bombe

Serves 8
Preparation time: 20 mins
Freezing time: 3 hours
4020 kcal/16820 kJ

---

*400 ml/**14 fl oz**/1³/₄ cups Pineapple Fruit Ice (page 16)*

---

*400 ml/**14 fl oz**/1³/₄ cups Rum and Raisin Ice Cream (page 24)*

---

*100 g/**4 oz** candied pineapple, diced*

---

1 Place the bombe mould in the freezer for 15 minutes.

2 Coat the mould with pineapple fruit ice and freeze for 30 minutes.

3 Prepare the rum and raisin ice as described, then when folding in the second amount of whipped cream, add the candied pineapple at the same time. Place inside the mould, filling it to the top and smooth surface with a palette knife. Cover and freeze the ice bombe for at least 2 hours.

Photograph (right)

Apricot and Brandy Ice Gâteau

Serves 10
Preparation time: 30 mins
Freezing time: 4 hours
5380 kcal/22510 kJ

---

1 × 20 cm/*8 in* layer sponge cake

225 g/*8 oz* orange marmalade left in the refrigerator overnight

450 ml/*³/₄ pt*/2 cups Apricot Ice (page 16)

450 ml/*³/₄ pt*/2 cups Brandy Parfait (page 44)

150 ml/*¹/₄ pt*/*²/₃* cup whipping cream, whipped

---

1 Place the sponge layer in a spring-clip cake tin and chill for 20 minutes in the freezer. Tip the marmalade into a dish.
2 Spread the apricot ice over the chilled sponge then return to the freezer.
3 Spread the marmalade thinly over the frozen apricot ice, mix the rest carefully with the parfait and add to the tin. Cover and freeze for at least 3 hours.
4 Turn out onto a plate that has been in the freezer for 30 minutes.
5 Spread a thin layer of whipped cream over the gâteau and garnish prettily with oranges and cream.

Photograph opposite (top)

Emperor's Ice Cream

Serves 4 to 6
Preparation time: 35 mins
Freezing time: 3 hours
2815 kcal/11820 kJ

---

30 ml/*2 tbsp* raisins

45 ml/*3 tbsp* Kirsch or fruit brandy

6 egg yolks

100 g/*4 oz*/*¹/₂* cup caster sugar

5 ml/*1 tsp* vanilla essence

grated rind of ¹/₂ lemon

3 egg whites

5 ml/*1 tsp* lemon juice

450 ml/*³/₄ pt*/2 cups double cream, whipped

cocoa powder

---

1 Soak the raisins overnight in the Kirsch or fruit brandy.
2 Put the egg yolks into a bowl with 75 g/3¹/₂ oz/*¹/₃* cup of vanilla essence and lemon rind. Stand the bowl over a pan of simmering water and beat until thick and creamy. Cool completely.
3 In a separate bowl, beat the egg whites and lemon juice until stiff. Add the remaining sugar and beat until very thick.
4 Drain the raisins well and fold into the egg yolk mixture with the beaten whites, the cream and a little cocoa. Pack into a ring tin, cover and freeze.

Photograph opposite (bottom left)

Walnut Ice Cream

Serves 6
Preparation time: 40 mins
Freezing time: 3 hours
2565 kcal/10730 kJ

---

3 egg yolks

100 g/*4 oz*/*¹/₂* cup brown sugar

a pinch of salt

30 ml/*2 tbsp* maple syrup

500 ml/*17 fl oz*/*2¹/₄* cups full cream milk

20 ml/*4 tsp* rum

250 ml/*8 fl oz*/1 cup double cream

5 ml/*1 tsp* vanilla essence

100 g/*4 oz*/*¹/₂* cup walnuts, coarsely chopped

---

1 Put the egg yolks, sugar, salt and maple syrup into a bowl. Mix well, adding the milk a little at a time. Add the rum. Beat to a thick and creamy mixture over a pan of gently simmering water.
2 Beat the cream until stiff. Stir in the vanilla essence.
3 Stir the walnuts into the egg mixture then fold in the whipped cream. Spoon into a freezer container, cover and freeze. Stir gently from time to time for smoothness.

Photograph opposite (bottom right)

29

Sorbets

As a refreshing dessert on a hot day or a cleansing dish between rich main courses, sorbets are the perfect thing to serve.

Redcurrant Sorbet

Serves 4
Preparation time: 20 mins
Freezing time: 3 hours
575 kcal/2405 kJ

---

75 g/**3 oz**/¹/₃ *cup caster sugar*

---

30 ml/**2 tbsp** water

---

400 g/**14 oz** *redcurrants, removed from stalks*

---

juice of 1 lemon

---

30 ml/**2 tbsp** *cassis (blackcurrant liqueur)*

---

1 Place the sugar and water in a small saucepan. Dissolve the sugar over a low heat, stirring. Boil gently until the liquid forms syrupy threads. Leave to cool.
2 Purée the redcurrants in a blender then rub through a sieve. Add the lemon juice, cassis and sugar syrup, stirring well. Cover and freeze in a bowl stirring several times while freezing.

Photograph opposite (top left)

Pear Sorbet

Serves 4
Preparation time: 30 mins
995 kcal/3995 kJ

---

4 dessert pears

---

120 ml/**4 fl oz**/¹/₂ *cup water*

---

75 g/**3 oz**/¹/₃ *cup caster sugar*

---

375 ml/**13 fl oz**/1¹/₂ *cups dry white wine*

---

1 egg white

---

1 Peel the pears, quarter and core them and put them into a saucepan with the water and the sugar and simmer gently for 10 minutes until soft.
2 Purée the pears and the liquid in a blender. Stir the white wine into the pear pulp, pour into a freezer container and freeze for 2 hours.
3 Beat the egg white until stiff and fold into the sorbet mixture. Cover and freeze for 2 hours, stir well to break up the crystals, then freeze until firm.

Photograph opposite (top right)

Melon Sorbet

Serves 4
Preparation time: 20 mins
Freezing time: 6 hours
705 kcal/2950 kJ

---

2 ripe honeydew melons

---

250 ml/**8 fl oz**/1 *cup water*

---

10 ml/**2 tsp** *honey*

---

100 g/ **4 oz**/¹/₂ *cup caster sugar*

---

1 Halve the melons and remove the seeds. Reserve.
2 Boil the water with the honey and sugar then leave to cool. Put melon seeds into the sugar syrup and leave to soak in the refrigerator for 1 hour. Rub through a sieve and discard the seeds.

3 Purée the melon flesh with the sugar syrup, place in a shallow container then cover and freeze. To avoid the formation of large ice crystals, stir well with a fork every 10 to 15 minutes.

Photograph opposite (bottom left)

> **Gourmet Tip**
> Soak small pieces of melon in a mixture of Campari, honey and lemon juice to serve with the sorbet.

Mango Sorbet

Serves 4
Preparation time: 15 mins
Freezing time: 6 hours
490 kcal/2050 kJ

---

4 mangoes

---

10 ml/**2 tsp** *icing sugar*

---

30 ml/**2 tbsp** *lemon juice*

---

15 ml/**1 tbsp** *brandy*

---

1 Purée the flesh of the mangoes then transfer it to a bowl.
2 Add the icing sugar, lemon juice and brandy then mix well. Pour into a freezer container, cover and freeze.
3 Beat the mixture every 30 minutes. Freeze until hard.

Photograph opposite (bottom right)

Champagne Sorbet

Serves 4 to 6
Preparation time: 15 mins
Freezing time: 3 hours
1390 kcal/5815 kJ

225 g/8 oz/1 cup caster sugar
250 ml;8 fl oz/1 cup water
juice of 1/2 lemon
450 ml/3/4 pt/2 cups Champagne or sparkling wine
2 egg whites
10 ml/2 tsp icing sugar

1 Place the sugar and water in a small saucepan. Dissolve the sugar over a low heat, stirring. Boil gently until the liquid forms syrupy threads. Leave to cool, then add the lemon juice and Champagne or wine. Pour into a freezer container, cover and freeze.
2 After 1 to 1 1/2 hours, beat the egg whites with the icing sugar until stiff and fold into the mixture.
3 Stir the mixture frequently during freezing.

Photograph (left)

Gourmet Tip
A particularly attractive way of serving a Champagne Sorbet is in tall, stemmed glasses, garnished with mint or lemon balm leaves.

Mint Sorbet

Serves 4
Preparation time: 25 mins
Freezing time: 5 hours
1450 kcal/6070 kJ

---

250 ml/8 fl oz/1 cup Sugar Syrup (page 16)

12 mint leaves

450 ml/³/₄ pt/2 cups white wine

juice of 2 limes

1 egg white

15 ml/1 tbsp icing sugar

a few chopped mint leaves

---

1 Heat the Sugar Syrup, without boiling, add the mint leaves and leave to soak for 20 minutes.
2 Remove the mint leaves. Stir the wine and lemon juice into the flavoured sugar and transfer to a container when cold. Cover and freeze.
3 Stir the sorbet mixture every 30 minutes from the edges to the centre in order to prevent large ice crystals forming. About 1 hour before serving, beat the egg white and icing sugar until stiff. Fold into the mint syrup with the chopped mint. Cover then continue to freeze, stirring occasionally, until hard.

Photograph (right)

Rhubarb Sorbet

Serves 4
Preparation time: 25 mins
Freezing time: 4 hours
410 kcal/1715 kJ

---

350 g/12 oz rhubarb

1 small blood orange

75 g/3 oz/¹/₃ cup caster sugar

120 ml/4 fl oz/¹/₂ cup white wine

---

1 Wash and clean the rhubarb, cut into short lengths and put into a saucepan. Peel the orange and coarsely dice the flesh. Add to the pan with the sugar and wine and simmer for 10 minutes. Cool slightly, then purée in a blender. Leave to cool and then chill well.
2 Spoon into a freezer container, cover and freeze, stirring fairly frequently to prevent the formation of large ice crystals.

Photograph opposite (top)

Red Wine and Peach Sorbet

Serves 4
Preparation time: 50 mins
Freezing time: 6 hours
1360 kcal/5690 kJ

---

4 ripe peaches

450 ml/³/₄ pt/2 cups red wine

1 stick cinnamon

2 cloves

a little grated orange and lemon rind

50 g/2 oz/¹/₄ cup caster sugar

120 ml/4 fl oz/¹/₂ cup Sugar Syrup (page 16)

1 egg white, whisked

---

1 Scald the peaches in boiling water, rinse with cold water and remove the skins. Halve, remove the stones and cube the flesh.
2 Simmer the red wine, spices, peel and sugar in a saucepan for 5 minutes. Strain, return to the saucepan then add the peach cubes. Cook over a medium heat for 10 minutes. Leave to cool.
3 Tip all the ingredients into a blender and work to smooth purée. Combine with the sugar syrup and freeze in a covered container until hard, gently whisking every 30 minutes.
4 About 30 minutes before serving, whisk again and fold in the egg white, whisked to a peaky snow. Continue to freeze.

Photograph opposite (left)

Pink Grapefruit Sorbet

Serves 4
Preparation time: 30 mins
Freezing time: 4 hours
740 kcal/3100 kJ

---

1 pink grapefruit

250 ml/8 fl oz/1 cup grapefruit juice

25 g/1 oz/2 tbsp sugar

120 ml/4 fl oz/¹/₂ cup double cream, whipped

1 egg white, whisked

30 ml/2 tbsp orange liqueur

---

1 Grate the rind off the grapefruit, place in a saucepan, just cover with water and simmer until tender. Leave to cool then rub through a sieve.
2 Halve the grapefruit and cut the flesh away from the pith and membranes, reserving the juice. Place in a bowl and add the grapefruit water and grapefruit juice. Add the sugar and stir until dissolved, then cover and freeze for 1 hour.
3 Beat the mixture thoroughly then freeze for a further 1 hour.
4 Stir the frozen sorbet mixture until well broken up then fold in the cream and egg white. Flavour with orange liqueur and return to the freezer.
5 Transfer to the refrigerator about 10 minutes before serving to soften.

Photograph opposite (bottom right)

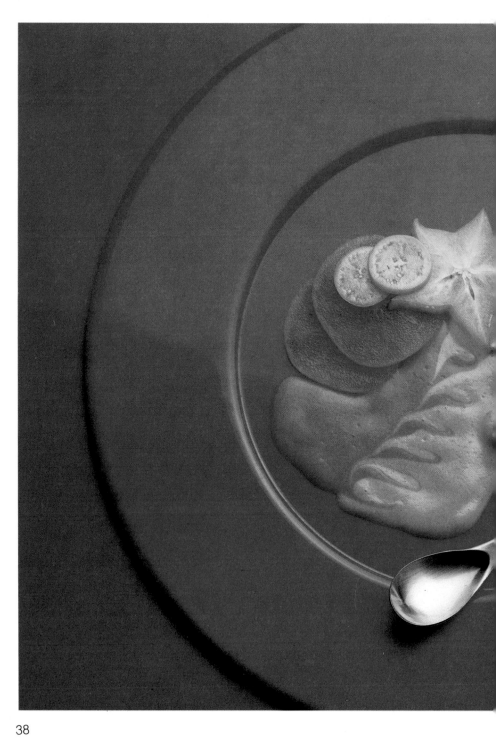

Parfaits

Creamy, fruity or slightly
tipsy, a parfait served
with a light sauce or
fresh fruit can be the
perfect ending to a fine
meal. If you take a little
extra care with the
presentation, they will
delight the eye as well as
the palate.

Summer Berry Parfait

Serves 4 to 6
Preparation time: 50 mins
Freezing time: 6 hours
1470 kcal/6150 kJ

50 g/2 oz/¹/₄ cup caster sugar

30 ml/2 tbsp water

4 egg yolks

150 ml/¹/₄ pt/²/₃ cup double cream, stiffly whipped

200 g/7 oz mixed berries (red and blackcurrants, raspberries, strawberries)

45 ml/3 tbsp cassis

30 ml/2 tbsp brandy

1 Put the sugar into a saucepan, add the water and dissolve over a low heat, stirring. Put the egg yolks into a bowl, gradually add the hot syrup and whisk until thick. Place the bowl in a sink or larger bowl partially filled with cold water. Whisk until cold and then fold in the cream.
2 Wash the berries, remove the stalks, then mix with the cassis and brandy. Fold into the egg and cream mixture.
3 Pour into a mould, cover and freeze until firm.

Photograph opposite (top)

Apple Parfait

Serves 4 to 6
Preparation time: 45 mins
Freezing time: 2 hours
2330 kcal/9750 kJ

225 g/8 oz dessert apples

50 g/2 oz/¹/₃ cup raisins

juice of 1 lemon

15 ml/1 tbsp caster sugar

2 pinches cinnamon

30 ml/2 tbsp Calvados

450 ml/³/₄ pt/2 cups whipping cream

10 ml/2 tsp icing sugar

6 egg yolks

1 Peel the apples, cut into small pieces and put into small bowl with the raisins. Sprinkle with the lemon juice, sugar and cinnamon. Pour over the Calvados and leave to marinate for 30 minutes.
2 Beat the cream and the icing sugar together until stiff then chill.
3 Add 30 ml/2 tbsp of marinade liquid to the egg yolks and beat to a cream in a bowl over a pan of simmering water. Place the bowl in a sink or larger bowl partially filled with cold water and continue to beat until cold.
4 Fold in cream and apple mixture. Pour into a mould, cover and freeze until firm.

Photograph opposite (centre)

Bilberry Parfait

Serves 8
Preparation time: 50 mins
Freezing time: 5 hours
3270 kcal/13680 kJ

4 eggs, separated

175 g/6 oz/³/₄ cup icing sugar

400 g/14 oz bilberries or blueberries

600 ml/1 pt/2¹/₂ cups whipping cream, whipped

juice of 1 lemon

1 Put the egg whites into bowl and beat until stiff. Add the icing sugar and place bowl over a pan of simmering water. Continue to beat until lukewarm. Cool completely, beating occasionally.
2 Whisk the egg yolks until fluffy. Purée the berries then rub through a sieve. Fold the egg yolks into the egg white mixture then stir in the berry purée, a little at a time. Finally fold in the whipped cream and add the lemon juice.
3 Pour into a mould, cover and freeze until firm.

Photograph opposite (bottom)

Cardamom Parfait

Serves 4
Preparation time: 35 mins
Freezing time: 4 hours
975 kcal/4080 kJ

---

seeds from 6 opened-out green cardamom pods

---

150 ml/¹/₄ pt/²/₃ cup double cream

---

2 egg yolks

---

40 g/1¹/₂ oz/3 tbsp caster sugar

---

5 ml/1 tsp rum

---

1 Bring the cardamom seeds and cream to the boil in a saucepan. Add the egg yolks, sugar and rum and mix well together. Rub through a sieve into a bowl, cover and freeze for at least 1 hour.
2 Beat the frozen mixture until smooth then pour into individual moulds, and cover and freeze for 2 hours.

Photograph (bottom)

Gingerbread Parfait

Serves 4 to 6
Preparation time: 45 mins
Freezing time: 3 hours
2900 kcal/12135 kJ

---

100 g/*4 oz* German
lebkuchen (chocolate
gingerbread)

---

30 ml/*2 tbsp* brandy

---

600 ml/*1 pt*/2¹/₂ cups double
cream

---

5 egg yolks

---

250 ml/*8 fl oz*/1 cup Sugar
Syrup (page 16)

---

1 Cut the gingerbread into small pieces. Purée in a blender with the brandy and 60 ml/4 tbsp of cream. Remove from the blender.
2 Put the egg yolks into a bowl with the sugar syrup and beat over a pan of gently simmering water until thick and creamy. Stand the bowl in the sink or a larger bowl partially filled with cold water and continue to beat until cold.
3 Stir in the gingerbread purée. Whip the remaining cream then fold it into the mixture. Transfer to a mould or bowl then cover and freeze until firm.

Photograph (top)

Drambuie Parfait

Serves 4
Preparation time: 30 mins
Freezing time: 5 hours
1735 kcal/7260 kJ

---

250 ml/*4 fl oz*/¹/₂ *cup sweet white wine*

250 ml/*4 fl oz*/¹/₂ *cup Sugar Syrup (page 16)*

4 egg yolks

75 ml/*5 tbsp*/1¹/₄ *cups Drambuie*

300 ml/¹/₂ **pt** *whipping cream, whipped*

---

1 Beat the wine, sugar syrup and egg yolks until thick and fluffy in a bowl standing over a pan of gently simmering water. Transfer the bowl to a sink or larger bowl partially filled with cold water and beat until cold.
2 Fold in the Drambuie and the whipped cream. Freeze in a deep, covered mould.

Photograph opposite (top left)

Poppy Parfait

Serves 4
Preparation time: 30 mins
Freezing time: 3 hours
3120 kcal/13055 kJ

---

30 ml/*2 tbsp poppy seeds, finely ground*

250 ml/*8 fl oz*/1 *cup milk*

6 egg yolks

150 g/*5 oz*/²/₃ *cup caster sugar*

450 ml/³/₄ **pt**/2 *cups whipping cream, whipped*

---

1 Simmer the poppy seeds in the milk until soft.
2 Beat the egg yolks in a bowl standing over a pan of gently simmering water until thick and creamy. Transfer the bowl to a sink or larger bowl partially filled with cold water. Beat until cold.
3 Fold the cream and poppy seed milk into the egg mixture.
4 Transfer to individual moulds, cover and freeze until firm.

Photograph opposite (top right)

Lime Parfait

Serves 4
Preparation time: 30 mins
Freezing time: 3 hours
1530 kcal/6400 kJ

---

1 egg yolk

100 g/*4 oz*/¹/₂ *cup caster sugar*

2 eggs

60 ml/*4 tbsp white wine*

juice of 3 limes

300 ml/¹/₂ **pt**/1¹/₄ *cups double cream, whipped*

grated rind of 1 lime

---

1 Mix the egg yolk with the sugar. Beat to a thick cream with the whole eggs, wine and lime juice in a bowl standing over a pan of gently simmering water. Stand the bowl in the sink or a larger bowl partially filled with cold water and beat until cold.
2 Fold in the cream and the lime rind, turn into a mould, cover and freeze until firm.

Photograph opposite (bottom left)

Brandy Parfait

Serves 6
Preparation time: 30 mins
Freezing time: 3 hours
2525 kcal/10565 kJ

---

4 eggs

100 g/*4 oz*/¹/₂ *cup caster sugar*

120 ml/*4 fl oz*/¹/₂ *cup brandy*

grated rind of 1 lemon

5 ml/*1 tsp vanilla essence*

a pinch of salt

450 ml/³/₄ **pt**/2 *cups double cream, whipped*

---

1 Beat the eggs, sugar, brandy, lemon rind, vanilla essence and salt to a thick cream in a bowl standing over a pan of simmering water. Transfer the bowl to a sink or larger bowl partially filled with cold water. Beat until cold.
2 Fold in the whipped cream, transfer to individual moulds, cover and freeze until firm.

Photograph opposite (bottom right)

Praline Parfait

Serves 4 to 6
Preparation time: 50 mins
Freezing time: 24 hours
2930 kcal/12260 kJ

100 ml/6¹/₂ tbsp water
100 g/4 oz/¹/₂ cup caster sugar
6 egg yolks
150 g/5 oz praline chocolates
50 g/2 oz dark chocolate
grated rind of 1 orange
45 ml/3 tbsp chocolate or coffee liqueur
15 ml/1 tbsp rum
1 large flake bar, crumbled
300 ml/¹/₂ pt/1¹/₄ cups whipping cream, whipped

1 Bring the water to the boil with the sugar. Remove from heat and whisk in the egg yolks. Bring briefly to the boil, sieve immediately and leave to cool.
2 Melt the praline chocolates and dark chocolate in a basin standing over a pan of simmering water. Stir in the orange rind, liqueur and rum.
3 Fold the chocolate mixture into the egg yolks with the chocolate flakes and cream. Pour into a mould, cover and freeze until firm.

Photograph (left)

Pear Parfait

Serves 6 to 8
Preparation time: 1 hour
Freezing time: 3 hours
2125 kcal/8890 kJ

*1 kg/**2 lb** ripe dessert pears*
*120 ml/**4 fl oz**/¹/₂ cup white wine*
*120 ml/**4 fl oz**/¹/₂ cup water*
*5 ml/**1 tbsp** vanilla essence*
¹/₂ stick of cinnamon
1 clove
*5 ml/**1 tsp** grated lemon rind*
juice of 1 lemon
1 egg
4 egg yolks
*50 g/**2 oz**/¹/₄ cup caster sugar*
*60 ml/**4 tbsp** pear brandy*
*250 ml/**8 fl oz**/1 cup whipping cream, whipped*

1 Peel and core the pears. Boil the wine, water, vanilla essence, cinnamon, clove, lemon rind and lemon juice for about 10 minutes. Strain, add the pears and simmer until soft. Purée in a blender.
2 Cook the pear pulp over a low heat until the liquid has boiled away, stirring frequently. Leave to cool. Beat the egg and egg yolks with the sugar in a bowl over a pan of hot water until thick. Transfer the bowl to a sink or larger bowl partially filled with cold water. Beat until cool.
3 Stir in the brandy, pear pulp and whipped cream. Pour into individual moulds, cover and freeze until firm.

Photograph (right)

47

Index of Recipes

foulsham
Yeovil Road, Slough, Berkshire, SL1 4JH

ISBN 0-572-01824-X

This English language edition copyright
© 1993 W. Foulsham & Co. Ltd
Originally published by Falken-Verlag,
GmbH, Niedernhausen TS, Germany
Photographs copyright © Falken Verlag

Printed in Portugal